VOCAL SELECTIONS from MACK & MABEL

MACK & MABEL

*The Musical Romance of
Mack Sennett's Funny and Fabulous Hollywood*

DAVID MERRICK
presents

ROBERT **PRESTON** BERNADETTE **PETERS**

MACK & MABEL

JERRY HERMAN

KIRK
with
JERRY DODGE   CHRISTOPHER MURNEY   TOM BATTEN
BERT MICHAELS   NANCY EVERS   ROBERT FITCH   STANLEY SIMMONDS
and
JAMES MITCHELL

In Association with EDWIN H. MORRIS

Scenery Designed By   Costume Designs by   Lighting Designed by
ROBIN WAGNER   **PATRICIA ZIPPRODT**   **THARON MUSSER**

Musical Director and
Vocal Arrangements   Orchestrations by   Dance Music by
DONALD PIPPIN   **PHILIP J. LANG**   **JOHN MORRIS**

Associate Choreographer   Production Supervisor
BUDDY SCHWAB   **LUCIA VICTOR**

Associate Producer   Based on an idea by
JACK SCHLISSEL   **LEONARD SPIGELGASS**

Original Cast Album by ABC Records

Directed and Choreographed by
GOWER CHAMPION

ISBN 978-0-88188-094-6

A PUBLICATION OF
EDWIN H. MORRIS & COMPANY
A DIVISION OF
MPL COMMUNICATIONS, INC.
http://www.mplcommunications.com

EXCLUSIVELY DISTRIBUTED BY

HAL•LEONARD®
CORPORATION

7777 W. BLUEMOUND RD. P.O. BOX 13819 MILWAUKEE, WI 53213

Vocal Selections from

MACK & MABEL

Contents

LOS ANGELES—ABC Records this week is releasing the original cast album from "Mack & Mabel," David Merrick's 86th Broadway production, which unites him with composer-lyricist Jerry Herman, author Michael Stewart and director-choreographer Gower Champion for the first time since "Hello, Dolly!"

The LP features 12 songs in addition to an overture, performed by stars Robert Preston, Bernadette Peters and Lisa Kirk, and was produced by noted arranger Sid Feller. In a departure from Broadway custom, it was recorded in split sessions on the Monday and Tuesday following its Sunday, October 6, opening, rather than, as is traditional, on the following Sunday.

The genesis of "Mack & Mabel" occurred three years ago when Herman was approached by Edwin Lester, of the Los Angeles Civic Light Opera, and the writer Leonard Spigelgass about doing a musical based on the ill-fated romance of Mack Sennett, Hollywood's pioneer of silent comedy, and the woman who he made a star, Mabel Normand. Herman and Spigelgass worked together for a year before Spigelgass departed to do a book on Edward G. Robinsdn (he retains credit for the show's idea), and Herman then collaborated with Michael Stewart under the Merrick auspices.

"Mack and Mabel" opened an eight-week engagement June 25 as part of the Los Angeles Civic Light Opera's 37th season and played short runs at the St. Louis Municipal Opera and the Kennedy Center in Washington, D.C., before arriving on Broadway, where it was greeted with critical acclaim. In the New York Times, Clives Barnes observed, "Mr. Herman is usually underrated by everyone but the public, but he has the common touch, a gift for melodies that seem at once familiar and memorable . . . in happy addition the musical collaborators here — Donald Pippin, Philip J. Lang and John Morris — know how to give a score that authentic Broadway gloss and brassiness."

Elsewhere, critical comment ranged from "A big, brassy, showbizzy musical" (Jeffrey Lyons, CBS Radio) to "A fast, rowdy musical" (Jack Gaver, United Press International) to "The most lovable musical in years" (Eugenia Sheppard, New York Post). In Variety, Hobe Morrison said, "Jerry Herman's songs are excellent — the most tuneful and lyrically suitable in years," and Rex Reed, in his New York Daily News column, added, "Jerry Herman has provided melodic songs, and nostalgic songs, and hit 'em in the stomach songs that are performed with imagination, wit and style by a vastly talented cast.

Perhaps William Glover, theater critic for the Associated Press, summed it up best. "What's better than splendid?" Glover wrote. Does terrific surpass enthralling? Let's not quibble. 'Mack & Mabel' deserves all the dandy adjectives around."

Applications for performance of this work, whether legitimate, stock, amateur, or foreign, should be addressed to:
SAMUEL FRENCH
45 West 25th Street
New York, NY 10010

Movies Were Movies

Music and Lyric by JERRY HERMAN

Movies Were Movies

Music and Lyric by
JERRY HERMAN

1. Mov-ies were mov-ies when you paid a dime___ to es - cape,
2. Mov-ies were mov-ies when Pau-line was tied___ to the track
3. *(Instrumental)* - - - - - - - - - - - - - - - - -

Cheer-ing the her - o and hiss-ing the man___ in the cape.
Af - ter she trudged___through the ice with a babe___ on her back.

Ro-mance and ac - tion and thrills,   Pard-ner, there's gold___ in them
Girls at the sea - shore would stand   All in a row___ in the

Look What Happened To Mabel

Music and Lyric by **JERRY HERMAN**

Look What Happened To Mabel

Music and Lyric by
JERRY HERMAN

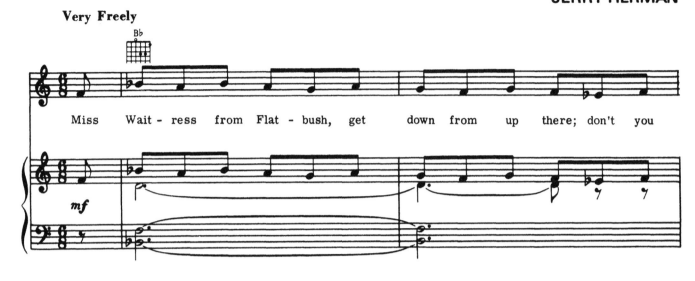

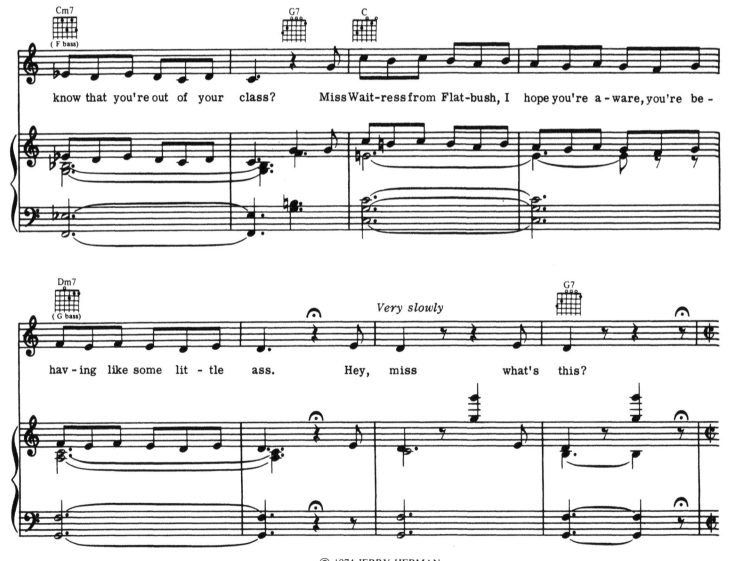

Big Time

Music and Lyric by JERRY HERMAN

Big Time

Music and Lyric by
JERRY HERMAN

Slowly and Freely

Moderate 4, (In Tempo)

The cher-ry on the top___ of the sun - dae,___ The shin - y star on top___ of the
This time we won't say, "Those luck- y bas - tards," This time those luck- y bas-tards are

tree. So you'd bet - ter grab it___ with your both hands___ when that
us. Ain't we some-thin'? Fare - well___ to the small time,___ to the

I Won't Send Roses

Music and Lyric by JERRY HERMAN

I Won't Send Roses

Music and Lyric by
JERRY HERMAN

I Wanna Make The World Laugh

Music and Lyric by **JERRY HERMAN**

I Wanna Make The World Laugh

Music and Lyric by
JERRY HERMAN

I'd rath - er film the guy____ with the fly on his nose.____ My
It deals with itch - ing pow - der and pa - pa's mus - tache.____ This

goal and my mis - sion, my burn - ing am - bi - tion is }
curse I've been blessed____ with, com - plete - ly pos -sessed____ with is }

I wan - na make the world laugh!

I wan - na make the world____

D.S. al Coda

Wherever He Ain't

Music and Lyric by JERRY HERMAN

Wherever He Ain't

Music and Lyric by
JERRY HERMAN

Hundreds Of Girls

Music and Lyric by JERRY HERMAN

Hundreds Of Girls

Music and Lyric by
JERRY HERMAN

When Mabel Comes In The Room

Music and Lyric by JERRY HERMAN

When Mabel Comes In The Room

Music and Lyric by
JERRY HERMAN

Time Heals Everything

Music and Lyric by JERRY HERMAN

Time Heals Everything

Music and Lyric by
JERRY HERMAN

Time heals ev - 'ry - thing, Tues-day, Thurs - day, Time heals ev - 'ry - thing
(Second time instrumental) -

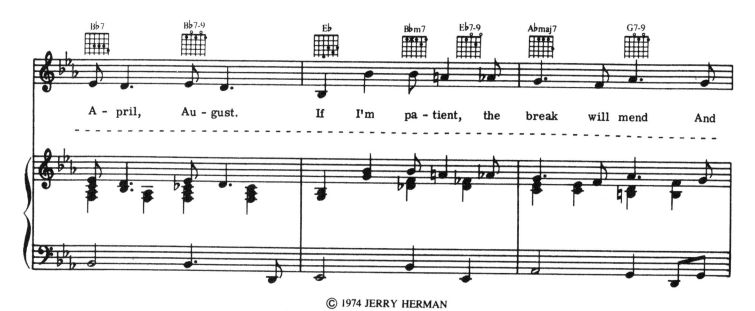

A - pril, Au - gust. If I'm pa - tient, the break will mend And

Tap Your Troubles Away

Music and Lyric by JERRY HERMAN

Tap Your Troubles Away

Music and Lyric by
JERRY HERMAN

Moderately Bright *(with a light touch)*

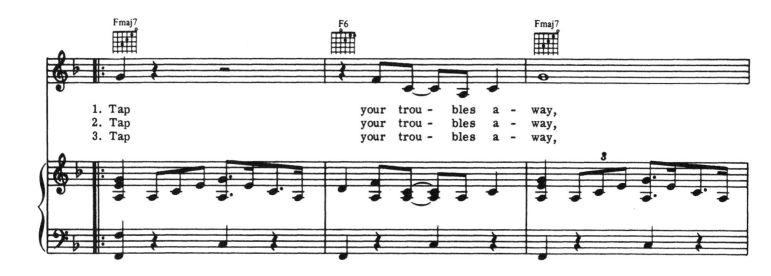

1. Tap your trou - bles a - way,
2. Tap your trou - bles a - way,
3. Tap your trou - bles a - way,

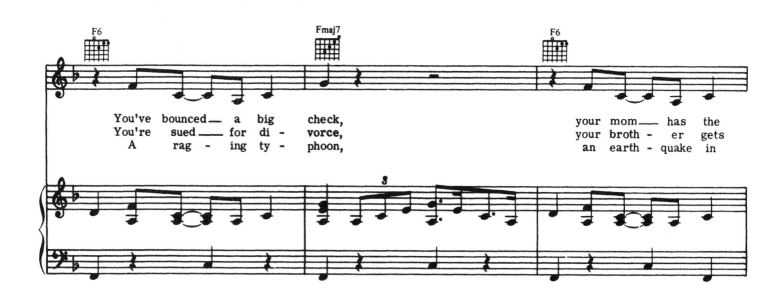

You've bounced _ a big   check,   your mom _ has the
You're sued _ for di - vorce,   your broth - er gets
A rag - ing ty - phoon,   an earth - quake in

I Promise You A Happy Ending

Music and Lyric by JERRY HERMAN

I Promise You A Happy Ending

Music and Lyric by
JERRY HERMAN

Tenderly

1. I pro - mise you a hap - py
pro - mise you a hap - py

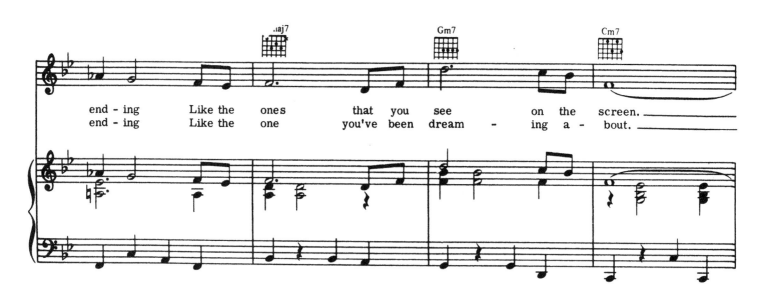

end - ing Like the ones that you see on the screen. ___
end - ing Like the one you've been dream - ing a - bout. ___